MW00904271

Artistic Adventures
DIARIES & JOURNALS

Kelly Burkholder

The Rourke Press, Inc.
Vero Beach, Florida 32964

PHOTO CREDITS
© East Coast Studios: cover, pages 4, 10, 17, 18, 21, 22; © Eyewire: pages 9, 14;
© Armentrout: page 13

PRODUCED & DESIGNED by East Coast Studios
eastcoaststudios.com

EDITORIAL SERVICES
Pamela Schroeder

Library of Congress Cataloging-in-Publication Data

Burkholder, Kelly, 1970-
    Diaries and journals / Kelly Burkholder.
        p. cm. — (Artistic adventures)
    ISBN 1-57103-352-1
    1. Diaries—Authorship—Juvenile literature. [1. Diaries.] I. Title.

PN4390 .B87 2000
808'.06692—dc21

                                                              00–028432

Printed in the USA

Contents

What Is a Diary?

Have you ever felt like nobody listens to you? Do you think no one knows how you feel? When you feel bad it is nice to have a friend to talk to. Friends listen to you. That is why you should have a diary. Writing in your diary is not like writing a letter or doing your homework. You do not have to worry about spelling. You do not have to worry about what others think. You write for you. Writing can help you grow. Your diary can help you learn about the kind of person you are.

Diary writing can begin at an early age.

MY CHORES

MAKE BED

TAKE OUT TRASH

SET TABLE

RAKE LEAVES

BOOKS I LIKE

SCREECH OWL
MYSTERIES

SONG OF THE SUN

DINOSAUR
DICTIONARY

Lists

Everyone makes lists. Our parents make shopping lists. We make lists of homework and things to do. A list can help you save time and stay **organized** (OR gan YZD). Your diary is a good place to keep lists.

Keep a list of the movies you see and the music you listen to. List the books you read and what you think about them. Lists help you put ideas together.

Keeping track of things on a list helps you stay organized.

Travel Diary

Are you going on a trip? You may want to take your diary. Write about your trip while you are away. Then later you will remember more. You will find that your **memories** (MEM uh REEZ) of your trip will be very **vivid** (VIV id). It's fun to travel and enjoy new things. It's also fun to remember your trip. A campfire or motel pool, someone you met—all of these are memories you can keep in your diary forever.

You can write about and save vacation memories in your diary.

Put the date at the top of your diary **entries** (EN treez). Write names of people you met and places you went. You may think you will remember everything, but you may not when you get home.

Memories of times spent with friends can be kept in your diary forever.

Creativity

Write your ideas down. You can collect them like rocks or dolls. An idea collection can help you create stories, poems, music, and drawings. Many writers, musicians, and artists use diaries to collect their **creative** (kree AY tiv) ideas. Remember, you can use anything you write any way you choose.

Many musicians keep their song ideas in a diary.

Feelings

Have you ever been angry with your brother or sister? Did you ever have a nightmare that scared you? Have you had a secret you didn't want to tell anyone? A diary is a good place to write about how you feel. It feels good to write about what makes you happy, sad, excited, or angry.

A diary is a safe place to write about how you feel.

Privacy

In your diary you may write things that you will not want others to read. You may be angry with someone. You might write something that is not very nice. You may have a secret that you don't want anyone else to know. That's okay. Your **purpose** (PUR pus) is not to hurt others. Your purpose is to write all about what you think and feel. Your diary is private, for you to read only. How can you be sure that others won't read your diary? You really can't be sure. Talk about your diary with your parents. Ask them to **respect** (reh SPEKT) your private diary. They may agree to read your diary only if you say it's okay.

This boy wants to keep his diary private.

Now and Then

A diary of your life creates a **record** (REK erd) of who you are, what you do, and what you think. Someday you may wish to share what you have written with others. Maybe you will keep your diary in a safe place until you are very old. Then you can give it to the next **generation** (JEN eh RAY shun) to read and enjoy. Imagine how much fun it would be to read about your parents or grandparents when they were children.

It is wonderful to hear stories from one generation to the next.

Get Started

Are you ready to begin? Write the day, date, and year on top of the page. Do this every time you write in your diary. Then you will be able to remember when something **occurred** (eh KURD). Start by writing about what is going on right now.

Your diary entry can be a few words or many pages. You can write big, small, neatly, or messily—any which way you want to write. It does not matter how you spell or how you sound. You are writing to make you happy.

You do not need to write every day. Maybe you will write every day at the beginning. Then you may write less often. If you keep writing, you will be able to see yourself grow. This is one of the great things about a diary. Now start writing and have fun!

A diary can help you remember the details of special events.

August 18

Today my dad took
us all out on a boat.
We went fishing.
Christian caught
a barracuda. It
had sharp teeth!

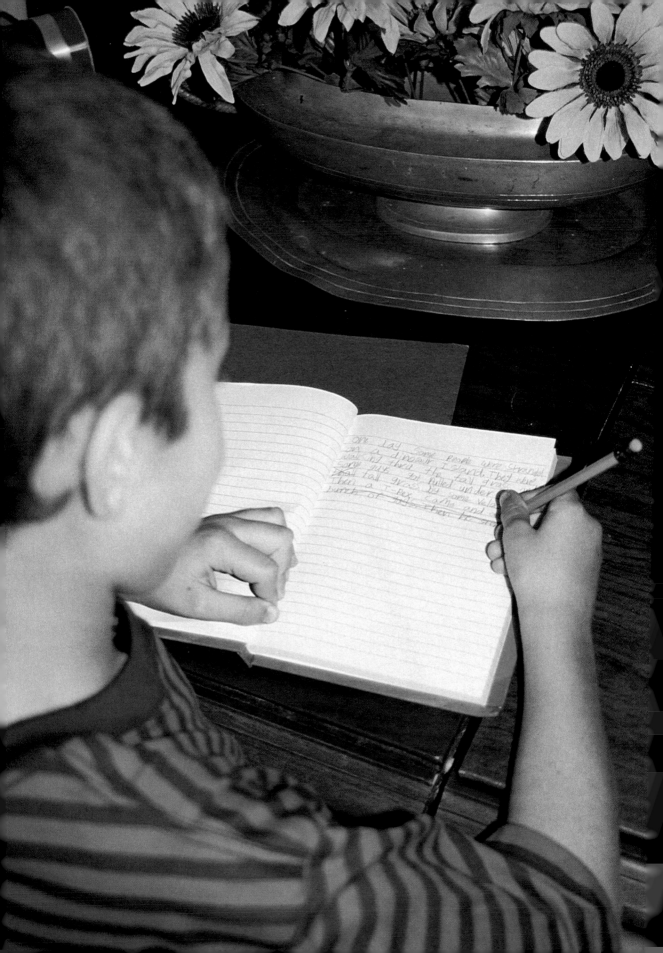

Glossary

creative (kree AY tiv) — using your imagination

entries (EN treez) — what you write in your diary each day

generation (JEN eh RAY shun) — a group of people about the same age; you are in the same generation as your classmates, and your parents are in another generation

memories (MEM uh REEZ) — pictures of the past that you see in your mind

occurred (eh KURD) — happened

organized (OR gan YZD) — to keep things in order

purpose (PUR pus) — why you do something

record (REK erd) — to preserve or keep in writing

respect (reh SPEKT) — to honor

vivid (VIV id) — just like real life, full of details

You don't need a reason to write. Just write anything you like.

Index

Further Reading

Find out more about diaries with these helpful information sites:

www.diarists.net
www.metajournals.com
www.TheSecretDiary.com
www.NationalJournalNetwork.com